HISTORIC HOMES OF PALMYRA TOWNSHIP
PIKE COUNTY
PENNSYLVANIA

HISTORIC HOMES OF PALMYRA TOWNSHIP PIKE COUNTY PENNSYLVANIA

Audrey Graybill

Wallenpaupack Historical Society
Paupack, PA

Copyright © 2011 Audrey Graybill

All rights reserved

ISBN 978-1-932380-09-5

Published by:
The Wallenpaupack Historical Society
PO Box 345
Paupack, PA 18451

Printed in the United States
Offset Paperback Manufacturing, Inc.
Laflin, PA

TABLE OF CONTENTS

TABLE OF CONTENTS	v
LIST OF ILLUSTRATIONS	vii
FOREWORD	ix
PREFACE	xv
KILLAM-PROBST-COLETTO	1
KILLAM-GUMBLE	5
KILLAM-DeFRANCO	11
PELLETT-COUTTS	15
WARNER-KIMBLE-SLOCUM	19
ANSLEY-VILARDI	25
VETTERLEIN	29
BUEHLER	33
ZIMMERMAN-REGA	37
ZIMMERMAN-WACKER	41
BENNETT-GUMBLE-COUTTS	43
KILLAM-WILLIAMS	47
CONRAD GUMBLE	51
HERMAN GUMBLE- SHIVE	57
FRANCIS SINGER	61
CASPER WISSLING - AUGUST SINGER	65
JACOB SEAMAN - LEWIS SINGER	67
FRASER SMITH - H.T. GUMBLE	71
QUICK - GOBLE	73
SIMPSON - ROBINSON	77
LYNN-KETTERING	81
BINGHAM-KILLAM-SIMONS	87
REFERENCES	89
INDIVIDUAL CONTRIBUTORS	91
ORAL HISTORIES	93
INDEX	95

LIST OF ILLUSTRATIONS

Figure 1 - Front View of the Colletto Home 1
Figure 2 - Colletto home showing large stone fireplace 2
Figure 3 - Front view of Killam-Gumble Home 5
Figure 4 - Wide Plank Floors - Common in many homes 6
Figure 5 - Window in Emil Gumble's House 7
Figure 6 - Stairs and Bannister in E. Gumble House 8
Figure 7 - 1925 Addition to Killam-Gumble Home 9
Figure 8 - Front View of Killam Family Home.................... 11
Figure 9 - Ground level fireplace in Killam home.............. 12
Figure 10 - Post and beam construction 13
Figure 11 - Front View of the Pellett-Coutts Home 15
Figure 12 - Pellett-Coutts Original Fireplace 17
Figure 13 - Front of Slocum Home................................. 19
Figure 14 - Former Post Office in Slocum Home............... 20
Figure 15 - Fireplace 21
Figure 16 - Joe Slocum and the Family Bible................... 22
Figure 17 - Cupboard in Slocum Dining Room 23
Figure 18 - Main View of Ansley Home 25
Figure 19 - Back View of Ansley Home 26
Figure 20 - Main View of "Maple Leaf Farm".................... 29
Figure 21 - Side View of Vetterlein Home 30
Figure 22 - Main View of "Idelwild Farm"........................ 33
Figure 23 - Barnyard 34
Figure 24 - View of Millpond from House 35
Figure 25 - Main View of John Zimmerman's Home.......... 37
Figure 26 - Remains of Barn Foundation and Stone Wall... 38
Figure 27 - Pattern Workshop....................................... 39
Figure 28 - Main View of Jacob Zimmerman Home........... 41
Figure 29 - Main View of Bennett-Coutts Home 43
Figure 30 - Main View of the Killam-Williams Home.......... 47
Figure 31 - Christmas Open House at the Williams House . 49
Figure 32 - Interior View of Exhibits and Bay Window 50
Figure 33 - Loom in the Back Room............................... 50
Figure 34 - Main View of Conrad Gumble, Sr. Home......... 51
Figure 35 - Interior Post Office..................................... 53

Figure 36 - Upstairs Bedroom in the Gumble Home 54
Figure 37 - Wardrobe built by Conrad Gumble, Sr. 55
Figure 38 - Staircase in Gumble Home built by Conrad Gumble 56
Figure 39 - Main View of the Herman Gumble Home 57
Figure 40 - Rubble Stone Foundation 58
Figure 41 - Hermann Gumble's Post and Beam Barn - Original Interior 59
Figure 42 - Singer House 61
Figure 43 - Door Leading to the Two-story Section of the House 63
Figure 44 - Main View of the Wissling Home, After the Addition 65
Figure 46 - Jacob Seaman Home 67
Figure 47 - Original Stone Foundation of Seaman Home ... 69
Figure 48 - Original Half-cut Logs Used as Joists in Seaman Home 70
Figure 45 - Frazer Smith - H. T. Gumble barn 71
Figure 49 - Alva Quick-Goble Home - 1919 73
Figure 50 - Original Quick's Machine Shed 74
Figure 51 - Main View of Robinson Home 77
Figure 52 - View of Privy at Robinson Home 78
Figure 53 - Side View of Summer Kitchen 79
Figure 54 - Front View of Lynn Home 81
Figure 55 - View of Half of the Front Parlor in Lynn Home. 83
Figure 56 - An Upstairs Bedroom Showing Heirloom Furniture 84
Figure 57 - Another Bedroom in the Lynn Home 85
Figure 58 - View of Bingham-Simons Home 87

FOREWORD

There are two threads to the history of land ownership in the Wallenpaupack Valley. One of them comes from Pennsylvania, the other from Connecticut. Unlike the Wyoming Valley, when these two conflicting claims to title came together, the battle was fought in the courtroom with words, not in the fields with guns.

The charter granted to William Penn was for the lands between the 40th and 43rd parallels of latitude, from the Delaware River west five degrees of longitude. Penn had to quiet any title or claim that others might have to that land. In addition to the Swedes already settled along the Delaware River, Penn had to deal with the claims by the native peoples. However, once those issues were satisfied, the Penns could do almost as they pleased with the entire colony. They sold some land outright. They retained other lands in large tracts called manors, which they intended to rent for continued income. The 12,150 acre Wallenpaupack Manor was but one of many of these tracts. Some authors have claimed it is the first manor, that honor belongs to Pennsbury Manor, patented in 1693. Others have claimed it is the largest manor, but the largest is Springettsbury with 64,520 acres. None of the Penns lived on the Wallenpaupack Manor, and there is not even any evidence any of them even saw the place.

While William Penn was apparently scrupulous about obtaining clear title from the Indians, and dealt fairly with them, his heirs were notorious for several bad faith deals and occasional outright fraud. The infamous Walking Purchase of 1737 has been described by many historians as a bad faith exercise, based on a treaty that may not have even existed. The Walking Purchase, and the treaty of 1749 annexed lands to the south of the Wallenpaupack Valley.

Both of them included land south of lines that ended at the mouth of the Lackawaxen River. The Penns' claim to the Wallenpaupack Valley officially started with the Purchase of 1768.

One measure of the Penns' bad faith is that they had the Wallenpaupack Manor surveyed for themselves on 14 October 1751 - seventeen years before they had clear title to it. The most charitable explanation for this is that they did not have an idea of where the northern boundary of the 1749 treaty actually lay. Most authors ascribe less innocent interpretations.

The Penns found there was little interest in the Wallenpaupack Manor. Until after the Revolution, there was plenty of good land in southeast and central Pennsylvania to satisfy the growing demand. However, there was a land boom starting in 1792 created by changes in land policy by the infant state government. James Wilson was caught up in the speculative fever, and bought the Wallenpaupack Manor (and several other large tracts north of the Manor) from the Penns. They held the mortgage. Wilson's enterprise to raise flax and sheep failed.

The Connecticut settlement of the Wallenpaupack valley began in 1763 with the arrival of three families from Connecticut. Although the evidence is sketchy and circumstantial, it appears the Carter and Duncan settlement was the opening round of a plan by the Connecticut based Delaware Companies to settle "their" territory. While the Susquehanna Company claimed the Wyoming Valley, the smaller Delaware Companies claimed the territory east of the Wyoming Valley to the Delaware River. After some scouting, it was apparent that the most likely spot for a large settlement was the Wallenpaupack Valley.

The treaty ending the French and Indian War had just been signed when Carter lead the group into the valley. The

French had encouraged the tribes of the Six Nations to attack English settlers, killing some, and taking others for ransom. The ransoming of English settlers proved to be a lucrative trade, and the Carters fell victim to the practice. When Carter and Duncan returned to the homestead and found their families murdered or taken, they raised a posse to pursue the Indians. When the posse caught up with a band of the Indians, Carter and Duncan were killed, and the posse fled. The Indians retreated into New York. By the time the Carter children had been returned to Cornwall, Connecticut, all that remained of the homestead was a low chimney. That chimney remained visible until the Lake flooded the site.

The next wave of settlers from Connecticut was larger, better organized and much better prepared to defend itself. There is more evidence that the 1774 settlement was the result of the Delaware Companies' planning. The surviving records of the Companies include many of the names of the 34 settlers as members. The move also parallels the settlement of the Wyoming Valley by the "big brother" Susquehanna Company.

Connecticut land rules were much simpler than Pennsylvania land rules. In Connecticut you took title to the land by occupying it and improving it. There was no land office to regulate surveys, collect fees and issue titles. If it was empty when you got there, you established a boundary by agreement with your neighbors, and settled. In the Wallenpaupack settlement, these agreements were most likely reached before the settlers left Connecticut, just as the Susquehanna Company did with the settlers in the Wyoming Valley.

Contrary to some histories, the Wallenpaupack settlers were not on their way to the Wyoming Valley. The records of the Susquehanna Company clearly list the names of the men who were moving onto specific parcels in the Wyoming Valley. None of the 34 original settlers is in those lists.

The settlement operated somewhat independently, but did have a local government under the jurisdiction of Connecticut. They appointed or elected individuals to serve in the various offices (justice of the peace, officers of the military company, tithing man, etc.) and reported these individuals to the colonial government. There are few records of where they all stayed when they evacuated the settlement after the Wyoming Massacre in July 1778, but they appear to have resumed their pre-war lifestyle when they returned after the Revolution.

Since the Connecticut settlers occupied the valley several miles southwest of the falls, and Wilson's attempt at settlement depended on the water power at the falls, the two groups did not collide. This prevented the outbreak of violence in the Wallenpaupack Valley during the Pennamite Wars.

However, when Wilson defaulted on the mortgage for the Manor, the Penns were forced to sue in court to recover title to the Manor. They sued Wilson's estate (he had died in North Carolina, fleeing from his creditors in an attempt to avoid debtors prison), and the Connecticut settlers, whom they considered squatters. The Wayne County court settled the matter by ordering the Manor sold. The new owner was required to sell the land occupied by the Connecticut settlers at market value based on a survey that confirmed their informal agreements on lot layout.

Samuel Sitgreaves (a lawyer from Easton who had once clerked for Wilson) bought the Manor. George Palmer (district surveyor) completed the survey, and formal Pennsylvania title to the land was issued to the original settlers, or their heirs, between 1805 and about 1812.

A few of the more affluent original settlers purchased tracts of land from the Commonwealth Land Office after the Revolution. Title to those lands is very clear. They made an application, received a warrant (hence the term warrantee tract) when they paid the initial fee, and got the final title (called a patent) when the survey was complete and the final fees were paid. All of these records are available in the State Archives in Harrisburg.

The vestiges of the Manor lines, the original settlers' lot lines and the boundaries of the warrantee tracts are still visible on modern maps. When Col Watres' Pennsylvania, New York and New Jersey Power Company assembled the land for the Lake Wallenpaupack project in 1911, most of the property lines at the outermost edge ended on the original Manor boundary. When the lands outside of the project boundaries were sold for development, most of those original parcels kept their identity. There are good examples of the original property lines. Whispering Pines development is the upland portion of Moses Killam, Jr.'s lot number 25 and preserves part of the Manor line. Lacawac Sanctuary preserves one corner and parts of two boundaries of the Manor (ignoring several recent additions). There are also instances where modern development has obscured the Manor. Tanglwood Lakes is an assemblage of parcels from the subdivided Manor, and the John Philips 128 warranty tract. One corner of the Manor is now an unmarked point in their recreation area along Kleinhans Creek.

It is fortunate for those who want to preserve the earliest houses of Palmyra Township that the early settlers wanted to work the fertile bottom land, and not waste it by building houses on it. They chose to lay out their lots so that everyone got a good strip of bottom land that ran up onto the higher ground. When the Lake was built, the house sites on the hillsides were spared from flooding. There were relatively few structures outside of Wilsonville that had to be razed to make way for the Lake. Most of the original homesteads that survived to 1924, still survive.

Settlement also took place outside the Manor, but not until early in the nineteenth century. Several of the original settlers bought land in the area from the Commonwealth Land Office. John Ansley bought several thousand acres in what is now Wayne and Pike counties.

The goal of this book is to put the oldest houses in Palmyra Township into the context of the history of land ownership in Pennsylvania. The map in the pocket insert is the best reconstruction of the original surveys done in 1805. It is based on the 1912 version of a map done by L. B. Stillwell of New York for the Pennsylvania, New York and New Jersey Power Company, the original developers of the Lake Wallenpaupack project, the Beers map of 1872, and modern data from USGS and the Pike County Tax Mapping Office.

PREFACE

As a young child growing up in Paupack, I was very interested in the stories my mother related about her family. Family was very important to her; all the neighbors were extended family to her and to each other. I was curious about the houses I passed and the folks who lived in them. As I learned more about the township as an adult, I thought it was important to establish a record of the township's oldest houses and their inhabitants. One of the things I hoped to determine was the identity of the oldest house that was still occupied. This proved not to be an easy task because I found that the hewn beams of a log cabin that were no longer suitable were dismantled and the materials reused in the foundations of newer, larger homes.

Some of the information included cannot easily be documented. For example, how do I know that Francis Singer was envied for his wine-making skills? This was family lore passed down to the next generation. Oral histories are a rich source of personal memoirs.

I am grateful to the Wallenpaupack Historical Society for enabling this book to be published. Several of the Directors joined me during my visits to the twenty-two homes. Their assistance and impressions proved to be invaluable. I am also grateful to the property owners who willingly allowed us to photograph the interiors and exteriors of these homes. Jean Hansen, Thomas Vilardi, Jill Porter, Nan Coutts Brown, Donal Coutts, were among those who freely shared their own research with me.

One of the historic homes was razed during the writing of this book. I was glad for the opportunity to visit the house the day before it was demolished. The current owners of the remaining twenty-one homes seem to have lovingly cared for these old places; renovations were done in a manner that preserved the integrity of the structure.

My thanks to Bruce Taylor for his helpful suggestions and to Jon Tandy for writing the Foreword and editing the manuscript.

Audrey Graybill
January 2011

KILLAM-PROBST-COLETTO

Figure 1 - Front View of the Colletto Home

Zadoc Killam, the patriarch of the Killam family, died before the lands of the settlement could be surveyed. Zadoc's three sons. Ephraim, Silas, and Moses, claimed his lands. Lot 2, the site of this farmhouse, was surveyed for Benjamin T. Killam, grandson of Zadoc and the son of Moses Killam, Zadoc's eldest son. Benjamin lived on Lot 2 for many years. According to Matthews in his *History of the Counties of Wayne, Pike and Monroe*, Benjamin, late in life, moved to Beemersville, near Gifford's Creek, which was further south along the present State Route 507. Killam, in his *1887 History of the Wallenpaupack Settlement*, says that Ben Killam lived on his farm until his death in 1872. He owned nearly 3,000 acres of timbered land when he died at the age of 74 years. Elizabeth Witter, his widow, sold a large tract of timbered lands (Mill Brook) to Joseph Atkinson who operated the saw mill at the time. The remainder of his lands passed to his youngest son, Marcus Napoleon Bonaparte Killam, who continued to live on Lot 2 until he purchased Lot 3 and moved his family to that place.

Figure 2 - Colletto home showing large stone fireplace

Benjamin T., a devout Christian, was a Methodist preacher, although possibly not ordained, who preached frequently in and out of the settlement. He officiated at many funerals and christenings and stood watch at many bedsides. Jean Gumble Hansen tells us that his friends referred to him, lovingly, as "Uncle Benny. A lane, known as "Uncle Benny's Lane" extended through the woods from his farm on Shiny Mountain to his brother's farm, Moses Jr., located on the Greentown Road (present State Route 507.)

In 1874, Atkinson sold 96 improved acres to Swiss emigrants, Jacob and Amelia Mahling. As the couple aged, the property was given to Joseph Schmidt, a German from Wurttenberg, who married Amelia Maeder, the Mahling's daughter or possibly their niece. The Mahlings lived at the (Schmidt) Smith house until their death. They are buried in the Old Paupack Cemetery.

Joseph and Amelia had seven daughters. Alfred and Edward Probst came to America from Switzerland in 1892, and by the 1900 census, Edward had married Josephine, the eldest Smith daughter. He was listed as the Head of Household. The Probst couple had six children. The three who married received property on the farm and built their homes there. The farm and farm house was retained by Rose, the eldest of the three unmarried sisters. Before her death, land was given to each grandchild. The remaining house property was sold to the present owner, William Coletto, who restored and preserved the house over a period of more than thirty years.

The house, built in 1810, according to a slip of paper glued on the inside of a corner cupboard, could claim to be the oldest house in the township. The original house boasts a large fireplace and baking oven shown in Figure 2. A second floor was added, with three bedrooms. Other rooms have been added to the house, and through modern renovations, the house has retained its charm. The bedrooms are furnished in antique furnishings, most of it original. The double planking of the house is exposed on the upstairs walls, showing clearly saw whorls on the 16" boards.

KILLAM-GUMBLE

Figure 3 - Front view of Killam-Gumble Home

This property may have been part of Lot 6 that was originally surveyed for Moses Killam. Its transfer of ownership is not easily determined. According to deed records, a Moses Killam deeded it to an Ephraim Killam and his wife, Harriet, who deeded it to Asher A. Killam and Powell C. Killam, grandsons of Moses Killam, Jr. The present double-planked house was built in 1817, according to Helen Killam Teeter who grew up in the nearby Killam house. Asher A. Killam sold to Marcus N.B. Killam, his third cousin, once removed. Marcus made his home at Mill Brook on Lot 3 and he gave this property to his son, Alfred E Killam.

Figure 4 - Wide Plank Floors - Common in many homes

The 1910 Palmyra Twp Census shows that Alfred's family was occupying the house at that time. A servant, Lizzie Peifer, and a boarder, Michael Duffy, also lived there. Alfred and his wife, Eliza, moved to Hawley and the Phillips family rented it for some time. By 1920, the farm was rented by Emil and Anna Burn Kimble Gumble and their five children. Emil purchased the farm from Alfred's sister, Esther Killam in 1924. She acquired it from Eliza Killam, Alfred's widow, as judgment for a debt.

Figure 5 - Window in Emil Gumble's House

The farm lands down to the river were sold to the lake developers. Esther moved to her own home on State Route 507 sometime after the death of her mother, Nancy Killam, in 1913.

Figure 6 - Stairs and Bannister in E. Gumble House

Emil and Anna Burn were married in 1902 in Hawley at the home of her uncle, Arthur Kimble. Emil, the youngest child of Conrad and Dorothea Gumble, made his living as a butcher. He was in business with his older brother, Fred. in Milford. It was said that they rafted cattle across the Delaware River. Anna Burn was a daughter of Andrew Jackson Kimble. Emil courted Anna Burn for many years, making the trip from Milford by wagon. He stayed overnight at the Kimble homestead, later known as the Slocum House.

In 1902, the Gumbles moved into the Gumble homestead in Gumbles and took over the job of postmaster from Emil's brother, Henry T. who was the first postmaster of Gumbles, PA. A small general store was set up in the dining room of that house. Their first child, Dorothea, was born there. Emil sold the property to Nora Del Smith, a school teacher hired to teach in the township schools. The couple then moved to Wisconsin but returned to Hawley when Anna Burn's asthma became too severe. After a period in Hawley, they rented the Killam farm, later buying it in 1923.

Figure 7 - 1925 Addition to Killam-Gumble Home

At some time before the Gumbles purchased the farm, a single plank, four room, two-story addition on the south side of the house was built to be used as servant quarters (see Figure 7). This part of the house was detached in 1927 and was moved a short distance to become a home for Emil's son, Jack and his wife, Jeanette, and their two small children, Clyde and Eugenia (Jean), During one particularly windy night, the young family scurried to their grandfather's house to sleep on the living room floor. Their house, still on the skids over the basement cavity, was in danger of being blown off its precarious perch. Later, Jack moved his family to a small house he built by State Route 507. It was built to be a gas station, but during the early years of the depression, the gas station was converted into living space.

KILLAM-DeFRANCO

Figure 8 - Front View of Killam Family Home

Lot 6 was surveyed for Moses Killam, Sr., son of Zadoc. Zadoc Killam, born in 1722, was fifty-two years of age when he first came to the Wallenpaupack Settlement. His two sons and one daughter probably married sometime between 1778 and 1783, the year of their return. Ephraim, the youngest son, married Abigail Bundy, step-daughter of John Ansley, and they may have married after 1783. Zadoc died sometime around 1800 before the lots were surveyed. His share was distributed among his three sons. Moses took Lot 6 and built his log house near the site of the present house. Moses lived seventy-two years, dying in 1831. His property passed to his eldest son, Moses, Jr. His other son, Benjamin T., received Lot 2 and was mentioned earlier.

Moses Jr. built a bigger home in 1812 on Lot 6. The log cabin of his father located in the present garden area was razed in 1826. Moses Jr. became the biggest landowner in the township and he provided farms for each of his sons. This house was passed to his son, George N. Killam, who, in turn, passed it to his children. The last Killam to live in the house was James Killam. Upon his death, the property was sold out of the family.

The Killam family, an influential and civic-minded family in the community, located the Red School on their farm near the road which crossed the river and continued on to Greentown. With the building of the lake, this road (modern Route 507) was re-located some distance to the south to its present location. For more information about the Red School and the other schools in the township, the reader is directed to Donal Coutts' *History of Palmyra Township* for a detailed account.

Figure 9 - Ground level fireplace in Killam home

Figure 9 shows large stone ground floor fireplace. On the outer wall behind this fireplace there was a second fireplace that was probably used as a summer kitchen. Remnants of the hearth stones can be seen. The bake oven was shared by these two fireplaces.

Above this fireplace on the ground floor, there is a second fireplace. A large addition on the south side had three additional fireplaces, two on the first floor and one on the second floor. Each fireplace has its own flue and shows beautiful stonework. It was customary for the Killam family to exchange the bedroom and the living room during the colder months of winter.

Figure 10 - Post and beam construction

The post and beam construction is evident through-out the house (Figure 10). The renovations have carefully preserved the beams. The house has been transformed to accommodate a modern family's lifestyle.

PELLETT-COUTTS

Figure 11 - Front View of the Pellett-Coutts Home

According to Ephraim Killam's account, John Pellett was 58 years old when he and his children and grandchildren came to the Wallenpaupack Valley; he was 67 years old when the Connecticut settlers returned permanently. He died at 86 years in 1801, long before the lots were surveyed, but he was the patriarch of an important family. As such, his family was allotted Lots 5, 8, 11, and half of Lot 12.

His daughter, Elizabeth, was married to the Revolutionary soldier, Phineas Lester, and this family settled on Lot 17. John Pellett, Jr. was the elder son and he received the lands that had been surveyed for his father. His brother, William, did not return to the Settlement in 1783 but remained in Orange County, NY. He is buried on Pellett's Island, near Goshen, NY, according to Killam.

John Jr. lived on Lot 11, located near the Indian Trail, also known as the Minisink/Wyoming Trail, and later the Salem Road. His log cabin, near the flats, was the scene of the Indian skirmish with the four young men, described in Killam's History of the Wallenpaupack Settlement. John married Nancy Bingham, daughter of Hezekiah, and together they had seven sons and two daughters. After 1783 when the Indian threat was over and the fort was no longer necessary, John decided to build a better house higher up the hill near the location of the old fort and the ever-flowing spring. That house, with many alterations, is known as the Pellett-Coutts homestead.

We are grateful to Nan Coutts Brown who has offered her research of the Pellett family for our use. It is from her research that we are able to describe the oldest section of the house. Could this be the oldest house in Paupack?

According to Nan, the first clue of the house's age is the "riven lath" construction that was used. "Riven lath was made by splitting thin saplings and nailing them closely together on the inside of exterior walls. A mixture of plaster was then applied to the riven lath. This was the method of construction that was used throughout the central part of the house that contained two tiny downstairs bedrooms, an attic-type bedroom (possibly originally a loft) upstairs, a kitchen, great room, a pantry and a stoop."

Nan continues her story, "however, one of the most compelling reasons to date the original house to the early 1800s is an exciting discovery that my sister, Faye, made in the spring of 2008. She was sitting in the living room one evening and, quite accidentally, noticed a date, '1807', painted on the living room fireplace right below the mantel! The black paint that someone had used many years ago to cover the old stone fireplace had gradually been fading and chipping off over the years and that evening, because the light was just right, Faye noticed this date, shining through the gold paint. According to Ephraim Killam in his history of the settlement, Hezekiah Bingham (Nancy's father) had inscribed the date '1801' on his chimney so Nancy may have carried on the tradition inside her own house."

Figure 12 - Pellett-Coutts Original Fireplace

John's sons, Guerdon and Calvin, divided the property after the death of their father. Guerdon took 151 acres on the southern half which he farmed and Calvin remained on the homestead. Guerdon had six milch cows in 1870 and reported in the Agricultural Census that he had produced 50 bushels of corn, 100 bushels of oats, and 150 bushels of potatoes. Upon his death, his son, Chester, took over the farming. Guerdon's eldest daughter, Susan, and her husband, Edmund Hardenberg, took ownership of a portion of Guerdon's holdings.

During Calvin and Eunice Kimble Pellett's tenure in the house, a major change took place. Calvin added a large Colonial addition to the front of the house in 1842. The front of the house now faced Ansley Road. Nan describes the addition. "The addition to the first floor consisted of a front 'parlor', a front bedroom, hallway and stairs to the second floor and a door and steps to the cellar. The second floor addition consisted of three additional bedrooms and the attic.' The kitchen in the rear was added later. "

Calvin was the first postmaster of Paupack in 1853. His son, Theodore, was named postmaster in 1857, and his brother, Guerdon, was named postmaster in 1870. The post office was situated in the Pellett home. In 1873, the Pellett property was sold to Marcus Napoleon Bonaparte Killam. Killam's son, Benjamin F. Killam inherited the house, 73 acres of improved land and 140 unimproved acres. Asher Killam, a cousin, managed the farm for some years, and according to Nan, assumed the office of postmaster from Frances Hollister Killam. In 1901, B.F. Killam operated a telephone exchange from his home.

The property passed from the Killams to Henry Weill and a number of future owners, during which time it fell into disrepair. A defunct "Paupack Camp" operated on the premises until probably 1939. When two brothers, George and Harold Coutts, purchased it in 1946, the grounds and buildings were a disaster.

Since their wedding in 1947, George and Christine Coutts labored to restore the house to its present condition. Years of love and elbow grease involving the entire family resulted in a home that truly reflects the efforts of all the past inhabitants. Besides establishing a home for their four children, they prospered in the resort business, contributed to their community, and continued the legacy of the early settlers.

WARNER-KIMBLE-SLOCUM

Figure 13 - Front of Slocum Home

Court records indicate that in 1850 Jonas Ansley sold a large parcel of Ansley land to Peter Warner. Warner, his wife, Hetty, and their four children farmed the land until 1875. Warner was a blacksmith and postmaster. In 1878 Warner sold his farm to Andrew Jackson Kimble, grandson of Abel Kimble. The Kimble family had been living with Nancy's parents at the nearby Pellett home; their daughter, Eunice, was born in the Pellett home. Jackson's first wife, Helen Pellett, had one daughter; after her death Jackson married her sister, Nancy, and that couple had five daughters.

Figure 14 - Former Post Office in Slocum Home

Figure 14 shows the size of the Post Office, now a part of a small bathroom. Neighbors picked up mail here until the Post Office was moved to the Pellett house.

After Jackson's death, Nancy deeded this property to her daughter, Eunice, and her husband, Joseph Slocum. The property stills remains in this family. The built-in cupboard (Figure 17) and the fireplace (Figure 15) in the dining room of the house complement the family heirlooms.

Figure 15 - Fireplace

Eunice and Joseph had two daughters, Frances and Katherine. After the early death of Eunice's sister, Helen, the Slocums welcomed her husband and two young children to live with them.

Joe and Eunice Slocum were important members of the community. Joe was well-known for his marksmanship. Their daughter, Frances and her husband continued living in the homestead. Their son and his family are the current owners of the property.

Two prized possessions of the Porter famly are a photograph of Joseph Slocum and a Slocum family Bible (Figure 16).

Figure 16 - Joe Slocum and the Family Bible

Figure 17 - Cupboard in Slocum Dining Room

ANSLEY-VILARDI

Figure 18 - Main View of Ansley Home

Major John Ansley, one of the original settlers to the Wallenpaupack Valley, held a position of respect and leadership in the Wallenpaupack Settlement. He served as the blacksmith, a vital role on any frontier, but he also had a military title and commanded the respect of the others. His holdings were Lot 13 near the location of the Fort, Lot 15 where the present house is situated, and he later acquired Lot 10, known as the Clark section. The northern part of Lot 15 was later sold to Jacob Kimble, Jr.

Major John married Eunice Meech Bundy, a widow with two young daughters, Abby and Eunice, in the Congregational Church, Preston, CT in 1763. The couple had three sons before coming to the Settlement. Joseph was born in Paupack in 1775. John, Jr. and Joseph made their homes on Lots 13 and 15, respectively. Major Ansley died in 1806 and he was probably buried in a family cemetery on his property.

His son, John who also had the title of Major, was buried in the Paupack cemetery, as were many of his descendants.

Joseph Ansley, his youngest son, returned to the Settlement and occupied Lot 15. He built the early parts of the present house. He farmed and operated an inn to provide traveling accommodations to travelers on the Minisink/Wyoming Road (also known as the Salem Road) which passed very near the house.

Jonas, Joseph's son, inherited the property. The property passed through six generations of descendants until it was purchased outside of the family by Tom and Lisa Vilardi.

Figure 19 - Back View of Ansley Home

The current owners, in the process of making repairs to the house and indulging in their love of history, have done considerable research into house construction, colonial technology, and the Ansley family history. Crawling around attic beams, floor joists, etc. several facts have been made apparent. There is evidence that parts of the Ansley House were built as early as 1790. When the settlers returned in 1783 to the area following the Revolutionary War and the last of the Indian troubles, they found fourteen log cabins standing, albeit in bad repair. The Vilardis have found evidence that the original logs, cut and squared, were incorporated within later construction. To quote the owner, "some clapboards of the older main portion of the house were removed. This uncovered large hand-cut beams with evidence of axe marks that were notched and pinned together with wooden dowels…the floor beams in the crawl space under the living room appear to be logs split in half…and the main beams in the cellar consist of hand-cut beams with the bark still on in places and smaller water-sawmill beams [are] notched into the larger hand-cut beams."

Vilardi thinks that the 1774 log house may have been incorporated into the living room of the newer house, since some of the beams are hand-cut and some floorboards are hand-planed. Is this the oldest house in Paupack? The question goes unanswered.

The log beams used in the original log houses were usable in 1783 when the settlers returned and started to put their homes together. The beams represented too much labor to be wasted and so they could be found inside many of the existing homes.

The Ansley family, like all of its neighbors, sold the land along the river to the developers who were intent on building the lake. With some additional cash, they, also like many of their neighbors, made major improvements to their property. To quote Tom Vilardi:

"In the late 1920's the house was enlarged to provide an additional four guestrooms, (bringing the upstairs number to 10), adjoining private living space for the Ansley family downstairs and two full and one-half bathrooms."

With the tradition of providing room and board firmly entrenched in the family's lifestyle, the twentieth century Ansleys continued the tradition of taking in boarders who wanted a few days in the country. Sunday dinner of roasted chicken was a community favorite and well-attended. When State Route 507 was improved and relocated so that Ansley Road was no longer the main thoroughfare, the road crew stayed in the Ansley Boarding House and worked around the clock, stringing up electric wires from the house to illuminate the new road bed.

The Vilardis plan to carry on the legacy of hospitality by opening a Bed and Breakfast in the old house and -so the "ghosts of past visitors" will welcome the guests.

VETTERLEIN

Figure 20 - Main View of "Maple Leaf Farm"

This property is part of Lot 15 and 16. Jacob Kimble Jr. received the northern half of Lot 15 and settled on this portion. He purchased Lot 16 and other property, increasing his holdings to 270 acres. Jacob's son, Hermann N. Kimble lived on the property.

Henry Vetterlein, formerly of Saxony, and his wife, Frederike, lived in New York City after first arriving in America, and he operated a feed store. They had one child, Walter, born in 1856. For reasons not known to us, they moved to Paupack and purchased Jacob Kimble, Jr.'s farm from Jacob's daughter, Esther Kimble. This farm was located near the entrance of Ansley Road. The Vetterlein family appears in the Palmyra Township Census of 1870.

Upon the death of his father in 1888, Walter inherited the farm. He had married Wilhelmina Buehler, a young woman who had come to America with her family in 1880. Her parents, Christof and Katherine Buehler, lived nearby in a farm near the Atkinson Farm and saw mill.

In addition to operating a large farm, the Vetterleins took in summer boarders as well. The farm was named "Maple Leaf Farm" because of the beautiful maple trees that surrounded the house. Known for great cooking, lots of fresh garden vegetables, and balmy breezes, the farm was a popular resort. With the building of the lake, the family sold the lower section to the lake developers.

Figure 21 - Side View of Vetterlein Home

Walter Vetterlein was well-known to the local residents because he served for many years as the magistrate or justice of the peace. His account book of these years has been given to the Wallenpaupack Historical Society and it reveals the ebb and flow of country life in the early 20th century. Walter died in 1929; Minnie died in 1941.

Walter and Minnie Vetterlein had six children; one child did not survive to adulthood. The family of Alma Vetterlein Mansuy retains the ownership.

BUEHLER

Figure 22 - Main View of "Idelwild Farm"

Joseph Atkinson took over the operation of the Killam/Kimble sawmill located on one of the branches of the Mill Brook. He situated his farm not far from the sawmill and created a large pond to provide water power. Atkinson's farmhouse was later owned by the Hanna family. This pond is now referred to as Buehler's Pond.

Christof and Katherine Buehler, his second wife, emigrated to America in 1880 from Meimsheim, Wurttenberg. They arrived in Paupack and lived near their married daughter, Minnie Vetterlein, in a second farmhouse on the Atkinson farm. This couple had one son, William, whose family continues to own the property.

When William married, he and his wife, Louise Timmerman, purchased the house from the Atkinson family in 1913. The peaceful setting in the woods, with the attraction of the pond, enticed people to spend a week or two each summer at the farm. The good cooking and solitude has prevailed and, in at least one case, five generations of a family have returned to Buehler's year after year.

William and Louise 's son, Paul and his wife, Virginia, continued the tradition of hospitality. After Paul's death, their son, Scott, joined his mother. The farm is currently leased and still operates as a resort.

Figure 23 - Barnyard

The barnyard has remained much the same
The mill pond in the background offers tranquility and amusement to the guests.

Figure 24 - View of Millpond from House

ZIMMERMAN-REGA

Figure 25 - Main View of John Zimmerman's Home

This house, in the Zimmerman family from 1887 to 1999 when the family sold to Raymond Rega, appears to be very old. The oldest two-story portion contains two rooms on each floor. There is no evidence of a fireplace or hearth. The upstairs left bedroom seems to be older and might possibly have been a loft. The supporting floor joists are whole or halved logs with the bark remaining; the floor boards are spruce. The floor of the upstairs right bedroom is made of hickory. Large roof beams are exposed and the ceiling is low. The privy was attached to the back of a nearby barn or carriage shed. According to information given to Mr. Rega when he purchased the property, the house was used for "migrant workers" who tended the cattle raised on the farm.

The farm extended to the river and stonewalls penned in the cattle. The foundation of a large barn is still clearly evident and shown in the photograph below. The barn was destroyed by fire and it was never rebuilt.

Figure 26 - Remains of Barn Foundation and Stone Wall

The farmhouse was occupied in the early 1900s by John, Jacob's son, his wife and five children. John operated a wallpaper business on the premises where he designed the rollers used for the patterns. The small building, shown below, was his workshop. Many wallpapering tools were donated by Mr. Rega to the Wallenpaupack Historical Society. They are currently on display in the Palmyra Township building on Gumbletown Road.

Figure 27 - Pattern Workshop

The land surrounding the farmhouse no longer resembles farmland. The trees have taken back the ground.

The house was used for many years as a vacation house.

An eat-in modern kitchen has been added, as well as a deck for outdoor living. An artisan well is located near the house. The house is a pleasant combination of the old and the new and serves as a perfect vacation getaway.

ZIMMERMAN-WACKER

Figure 28 - Main View of Jacob Zimmerman Home

Located on State Route 507, the former farmhouse of Jacob Zimmerman is hidden from view by tall evergreens. The barn, located across the road, is more clearly visible. It is one of three post and beam barns in the township, and in the 1960s served as a stable for saddle horses. The farmhouse has been sided and its appearance changed greatly through years of renovation.

Jacob Zimmerman emigrated from Switzerland in 1882 at the age of forty-six. A year later he was joined by his son, John (b.1869) and his daughter, Elsie (b.1875). According to courthouse records, Jacob purchased his property from Samuel Widner in 1887. Widner had purchased the land a few years earlier from Samuel Pellett. It is not known whether Zimmerman built the house. This family appears first on the 1900 Census of Palmyra Township, with the addition of a grandson, Jacob Brown (b.1897). Jacob arrived as a widower, but by 1910 he had married Margaret Steinman. By 1910, John, his son, is listed as the Head of Household for a second Zimmerman farm, located across the road and currently owned by Raymond Rega.

BENNETT-GUMBLE-COUTTS

Figure 29 - Main View of Bennett-Coutts Home

Nathaniel Gates brought his family to the Wallenpaupack Settlement in 1774. His daughter, Mary, was ten years old at the time. Mary has an important part in the story of the Settlement because it was she who discovered a small group of Tories hiding in the grasses near the river as she searched for the family cow. In Killam's account, "She {Mary} communicated the fact to some of the Settlers, who informed the officers... Jonathan Haskel was sent with a number of men in pursuit and soon succeeded in capturing them, eighteen in number. They proved to be deserters from the American army."

Gates returned with his family in 1783 and claimed Lot 24. He remained for a few years and then sold his holding to his daughter, Mary, and her husband, Stephen Bennett. When the survey was complete, Stephen Bennett occupied Lot 24, a parcel of 208 acres.

Stephen and Mary had six sons and two daughters. Of the sons, Jared, Lebbius, and Isaac K. lived on Lot 24; the others settling elsewhere. The brothers may have divided the acreage. Old deeds indicate that Jared and Isaac K. lived close to the river near what became Nemanie Lodge. Isaac lived to the left and Jared lived to the right. Lebbius died in 1863 at the age of sixty and his wife sold her portion of the farm to Conrad Gumble, Jr. in 1883, prior to her death. For a number of years before its sale, the house was occupied by Henry Edwards and his wife, Caroline Kimble. One can assume that the original farmhouse of Conrad Gumble was the earlier home of Lebbius Bennett.

Isaac K. married Augusta Beam for his second wife; they had one son, Henry. As Isaac's widow, Augusta and her son lived on the western portion of the Bennett Lot and they were neighbors to the Gumbles. Stephen Bennett, Jared's son from his second marriage, sold his father's holdings to Conrad Gumble in 1893. Conrad now owned Jared's and Lebbius' portions which combined into a large farm.

Conrad and Anna Grathwohl Gumble filled the house with ten sons and one daughter. As the boys reached adulthood and found jobs scarce in the area, several decided to try their luck in Wisconsin. Conrad eventually sold his rich river lands to the lake developers and, with the construction of the lake, lumbering jobs became plentiful, drawing some of the boys back home. With all the cut lumber and the need for more houses, the Gumble brothers formed a thriving building construction business. Many of the sons built their homes on the farm. With Anna's death, Conrad asked his daughter, Anna, and her husband, George Coutts, to return from Wisconsin to keep house for him at the farm. The farmhouse was once again filled with children. Anna and George Coutts had eight sons and one daughter.

According to George Coutts, Jr., the original farmhouse was nearly square with a porch on four sides. The hand-dug cellar was quite shallow with little headroom. A wing was added to the original section to accommodate the large family. In recent years, Robert Coutts raised the original part when he and his wife occupied that section of the house, finally giving adequate headroom to the cellar.

In their oral histories, both George, Jr. and Albert related what their life growing up on the farm was like. During World War II, when George, Harold and Robert saw active duty, Albert, at 17, took over the management of the farm. Later, Robert and his wife, Helen, lived in one half of the house and Anna and her son, Eugene, lived in the other half.

The Coutts farmhouse remains in the Coutts family. The farmhouse, surrounded by fields and orchards, is in a beautiful pastoral setting, rarely seen in this area. For many years, the Coutts family supplied eggs, milk, garden vegetables, and other farm products to the community.

KILLAM-WILLIAMS

Figure 30 - Main View of the Killam-Williams Home

Lot 25 was surveyed for Uriah Chapman, one of the first settlers. He was an elderly man at the time of the survey, and with his death in 1816, his lands passed to his son, William and his wife, Rachel Willis. William lived some years on Lot 25. Wishing to move to Ohio, William sold his land to one of the settlement's wealthiest landowners, Moses Killam, Jr. Moses and his wife had a large family of five sons and ten daughters. He was a large land owner and a partner in the Atkinson sawmill on Mill Brook. He was able to provide tracts of land to his five sons. Lot 25 he gave to his eldest, Dan D. and his wife, Margaret Rohrbacker, who took up residence there when they first married in 1835. The oldest portion rests on a dry stone foundation. Its second floor may well have been a loft over a common room.

Dan D's family grew to eleven and the structure needed to be expanded. A two-story addition was added in the mid-nineteenth century. Dan D. died in 1876; his widow died in 1881. Moses, the eldest son, inherited the property (250 acres) but he sold it to three of his siblings for $4,000. The house was further modernized in the 1880s when the daughter, Lucy, and her husband, Charles Williams, moved in with their family. Lucy's brother, Clay, sold his share to Lucy and her sister, Hellen, for $2,000 worth of timber. Hellen eventually ceded her rights to her sister.

The Williams operated a farm on the location. A large barn and several outbuildings completed the holdings. Upon Lucy's death, the house passed to her husband and two of their three children who remained unmarried. Marion, the married daughter, was to receive a cash settlement. The Williams farm extended to the river and the family received a sizeable settlement when the lower section was sold to the lake developers. With this added cash, the family made extensive renovations to the house. These included removing a small room in the front of the house to make room for a distinctive wrap-around porch; relocating an interior staircase in the main section and opening the downstairs into two large rooms. Central heating was installed and windows were added to the front room- all of which changed the farmhouse into a distinctive landmark..

The property remained in the family until the death of Ralph, in 1967. It passed to a great-nephew who, after several years, sold it to the CWDJS Associates for a housing development. In 2004, the developers donated the house and two acres of land to the fledgling Wallenpaupack Historical Society for use as a Museum/House.

Since accepting ownership, the WHS has been painstakingly stabilizing and restoring the house through the generous donations of its supporters. A new roof was installed and some drainage problems were resolved. The windows in the main rooms were stripped and stained. The ceiling was replaced and the walls were painted. Recently, a small

bathroom was modified to accommodate the handicapped, and renovations were made to the small kitchen. Handicapped parking, driveways, entrances and stair railings were installed.
.
Today, three rooms downstairs contain local donated artifacts, photographs, and examples of furnishings of the late nineteenth and early twentieth centuries.
Many donated articles are stored for future exhibits; a large collection of local photographs is being maintained. The house is open to visitors in the summer.

Figure 31 - Christmas Open House at the Williams House

Figure 32 - Interior View of Exhibits and Bay Window

Figure 33 - Loom in the Back Room

CONRAD GUMBLE

Figure 34 - Main View of Conrad Gumble, Sr. Home

In 1852, Conrad Gumble purchased fifty-one acres of land owned by Rudolphus Bingham. This was part of the land surveyed to Hezekiah Bingham (Lot 29) and Jacob Kimble (Lot 30). After establishing a successful sawmill on the Mill Brook in the southern end of the settlement, Jacob built a second sawmill, which he called Mill Brook Two on the Sheridan Stream that flowed to the river through the southeastern part of Lot 30. He built a cabin near the mill and lived in that location for several years. Rudolphus Bingham, son of Hezekiah Bingham, inherited some of the land owned by his father.

Conrad Gumble emigrated from Zennern, in the state of Kassel, Germany, in 1846 and he joined his elder brother, Hermann, who had arrived in America two years earlier. The brothers settled in Astoria, New York, and prospered in a popular business of painting woodland scenes on indoor blinds. It is highly possible that they met Francis Singer who told them of homesteading lands available in Pennsylvania and who encouraged them to be his next-door neighbors.

Conrad had purchased the land for $204 in 1852 and shared the property with his brother. In 1865, Conrad sold twenty-one acres to his brother for $102; in 1866, he purchased an additional twenty-one acres to add to his holdings. The two brothers worked together clearing the fields and building their houses. Conrad's family lived in the cabin just below the present house from 1858 to the early seventies when he built the present two-story frame house. The couple raised eleven children in this house; the nine boys sleeping upstairs in the loft, and the two girls sleeping in a small room in the back. After the birth of their last child, the family moved into the new structure.

The new farmhouse was well-built; it features five bedrooms upstairs which were sometimes rented to summer boarders as the children left home. The downstairs has a large dining room that served as a general store in the early 1900s. A parlor and a small bedroom, a central staircase, and a commodious kitchen make up the rest of the house. The kitchen boasted two side porches, an add-on pantry with the entrance to the wine cellar below, four windows with beautiful views of the valley, and later, Lake Wallenpaupack, and seven doors leading to other parts of the house.

In the 1870 Agricultural Census, the Gumble farm had three milch cows, two oxen, and one pig. The fields yielded twelve bushels of rye, forty bushels of corn, ninety bushels of buckwheat, and one hundred bushels of potatoes. This could be considered subsistence farming with anything extra used for barter or trade.

Figure 35 - Interior Post Office

Conrad died in 1898 from head injuries suffered in a fall down the cellar steps. His wife, Dorothea, died three months later. The farm was occupied by Conrad's son, Henry T. and his wife, until 1900 when Henry purchased the Smith farm about one-half mile to the east. Henry was named postmaster of "Gumbles" post office in 1900. The name was later changed to Gumbletown. Henry sold the homestead to his youngest brother, Emil. Emil and Anna Burn Gumble continued to operate the post office (Figure 35) at Gumbles and to run a general store.

The house remained in the Gumble family until 1914 when it was sold to Nora Del Smith, a school teacher from New York City. Nora Del taught in the township's one-room schools and continued to operate the post office. In 1918, she married Henry Gumble, recently widowed. The couple had one daughter.

The farm is well-known today for its picturesque view of the lake and the mountains beyond, as well as the attractive farmhouse and barn. It is carefully maintained by Nora Del's granddaughter and her family who enjoy it as a summer getaway. Several pieces of original furniture built by Conrad Gumble remain in the house. The newel post and stairway as well as a large wardrobe show his craftsmanship. A high-backed bed remains in the north bedroom.

Figure 36 - Upstairs Bedroom in the Gumble Home

Figure 37 - Wardrobe built by Conrad Gumble, Sr.

Figure 38 - Staircase in Gumble Home built by Conrad Gumble

HERMAN GUMBLE- SHIVE

Figure 39 - Main View of the Herman Gumble Home

Hermann Gumble, the elder brother of Conrad, accompanied his brother to Paupack (circa 1854) and worked side by side to clear the land. Hermann did not actually own his property until 1865. The original house, which was probably similar to Conrad's first home, burned and a second house was built on the site. The oldest part had a dry-stone foundation which can easily be seen today (Figure 40).

The house had many charming features, such as a graceful parlor bay window on the southwestern side. It was shaded by a large grape arbor. There was a large front porch oriented to the east; the front door opened to a staircase and a central hall led back to the kitchen. The ever-flowing spring is downhill from the kitchen and the privy.

Figure 40 - Rubble Stone Foundation

The topography of the land was sloped and the soil stony. According to the 1870 Census, the farm yielded rye, corn, buckwheat, and sixty bushels of potatoes. Hermann planted apple, pear, and peach trees which are still producing fruit today. He produced ten pounds of beeswax and one hundred pounds of honey in 1870.

Hermann married fifteen year-old Barbara Kastler in New York City in 1852. Their first child and only son, Charles Conrad, was born a year later. Five daughters followed. Barbara Kastler Gumble died at the age of thirty. Hermann died in 1897 and the property passed to his son, "C.C", who lived there with his wife, Annie Gessner of Blooming Grove, and their one son and five daughters.

Charles Conrad (C.C.) was reluctant to make any changes and the farm and house remained virtually without modernization. Upon his death, the property passed to his two unmarried daughters, Edith and Marie, who lived and worked in New York City. They eventually retired to the house and continued their father's resistance to change.

Upon their death, the house passed to a niece who sold the property to the family of Franklin Shive, long-time residents of Colony Cove North, Tafton. The Shives have given the old house some new life by stabilizing the house, landscaping the area around it, and enjoying its tranquility on the occasional weekend.

The barn shown here is one of the oldest in the township. The original barn was destroyed by fire and the neighbors rebuilt it in a few days. It is a post and beam structure. The original outer boards were removed and replaced several years ago, but the interior remains the same.

Figure 41 - Hermann Gumble's Post and Beam Barn - Original Interior

FRANCIS SINGER

Figure 42 - Singer House

Francis Singer emigrated from Urnegarten, Baden, Germany, and purchased land, in partnership with Jacob Seaman, in 1850. It is believed that he acted as a land agent, encouraging newly-arrived immigrants from Germany to homestead on land in the Wallenpaupack Manor. It is possible that he also convinced the Gumble brothers two years later to leave Astoria, New York, and to purchase land near his property.

Francis was familiar with the area, having purchased land in Greene Township in 1848. In 1850, he purchased land in Palmyra Township in partnership with Jacob Seaman. Both men built their homes across the road from each other. In 1855 at the age of thirty-seven, Francis married Auguste Berthe Frank of Blooming Grove (Zeladin, Saxony). Auguste was fifteen when she married; their first child, Lewis, was born the following year. Fifteen children were born to the couple in their marriage.

Singer hand-dug a cellar and used plentiful local stones as a foundation. Hand- adzed beams and half trees, with the bark remaining, supported a small double-planked common room with a back kitchen. He then added a one and one-half story. The dirt cellar still contains several wooden bins for vegetables. The stairway to the kitchen remains as well as the door to the other part of the house (Figure 43). The house, built on a downward slope, had a beautiful vista of the river valley and beyond. Cool breezes cleared the air in the summer months and cold blasts blew through the house in the winter months. The chicken coop, the orchard, and the barn were located below the house which was situated quite close to the dirt road.

Singer planted fruit trees which still stand today. His grape vines were a source of pride for he was well-known for his wine. For the 1870 tax report, Francis Singer declared 2 milch cows, 1 other cattle, 1 swine, 10 bushels of rye, 20 bushels of Indian corn, 20 bushels of buckwheat, 40 bushels of Irish potatoes, 160 pounds of butter, 20 bushels of orchard products, and 4 tons of hay. Much of the ground was hilly and rocky; the upper hills were suitable for some crops such as grains and potatoes. Like his neighbors, Singer was a subsistence farmer, selling or bartering surplus crops.

Figure 43 - Door Leading to the Two-story Section of the House

After the death of Francis, his youngest son, William, remained on the farm until it was sold to the Darbys in 1938. Will and his wife moved into a small cottage near the farm spring. Francis, Jr. "Schuster" had property adjoining the farm. His daughter, Esther and husband, Charles Gumble, built a house and lived there until the mid 30s. His son, August Singer, purchased the Wissling property across the road; his son, Lewis, purchased the Seaman farm, and his son, George, acquired considerable lands on the upper levels. His son, John (Jum) lived out his last years in a cabin near his brother, Will. Charles Singer, his other son, purchased land in Tafton near the river, in the vicinity of the modern Ehrhardt's Restaurant.

The farm remained in the family until sold to Earle and Bertha Darby in 1938. Earle had spent several years of his childhood in Paupack with his aunt and uncle, Elizabeth Snell Gumble and Henry T. Gumble. The property eventually passed to his daughter, Ethel Wohlfart, and to his granddaughter, Margaret Reidenbach, and most recently to his great-grandson, Mark Reidenbach, the current owner.

CASPER WISSLING - AUGUST SINGER

Figure 44 - Main View of the Wissling Home, After the Addition

Located directly across Gumbletown Road from the Francis Singer homestead was the homestead of Casper Wissling (Whistling) and his wife. Magdelena. Casper left Switzerland in 1854 and purchased the land from Francis Singer in the same year. It is assumed he began to build the current house right away.

The oldest part of the house (pre Civil War) is the only part with a hand-dug cellar and laid stone walls. It has the ceiling beams with the bark attached that were in common use at that time. It is located in the front left end of the house. The right side was added later, and still later, the wing in the back. It is necessary to imagine the old structure because the house has been sided and a porch added.

In the 1870 Township Agricultural Census, Wissling is said to have owned forty acres, seven of them improved. He owned one milch cow and two oxen and produced 18 bushels of rye, 20 bushels of corn, 9 bushels of buckwheat, and 30 bushels of potatoes.

Francis Singer bought the property back from Wissling. Francis' son, August, purchased the house and moved his family to that location after his farmhouse, near Seeley's in Tafton, burned. August died in 1933, and after the death of his widow, Anna Delling Singer, the property reverted to his estate. The children received a portion of his holdings and the house was retained by an unmarried daughter, Martha M., who shared the house with a younger sister, Erma Singer Box, whose son, Darryl Box, still owns the house.

JACOB SEAMAN - LEWIS SINGER

Figure 45 - Jacob Seaman Home

In 1850, Jacob Seaman and Francis Singer jointly purchased one hundred acres of the Manor Tract from Granville John Penn and Richard Penn through their attorney, George. Cadwalader, for three hundred dollars. The land was on both sides of the roadway leading to Big Pond or Lake Arthur (Fairview Lake). Seaman built his house on the south side of the road, slightly east of the Francis Singer homestead.

The house is located close to the present roadway on a steep slope; the farmland reaches to the higher level in the rear. The house follows the pattern of a hand-dug, laid stone cellar with split tree joists supporting a rectangular room at ground level which was probably divided into two small rooms. A small porch in front completed the homestead.

The original stone foundation, with some cement added later, is clearly visible in the basement level.

The floor joists are the original half-round trees that were accessible and manageable. The bark was not removed. A later owner added milled joists that are familiar today for added support.

This use of split young trees as joists was quite common during the 1850s. Several homes in the immediate area used these materials.

In the 1870 Census, Seaman owned fifty acres, thirty-five of them were unimproved. He owned one milch cow and two working oxen; he produced 6 bushels of rye, 25 bushels of corn, 63 bushels of buckwheat and 33 bushels of potatoes.

Jacob and Wilhelmina Seaman had two daughters, Helen and Matilda. Jacob died in 1876 at the age of fifty six. Lewis Singer, eldest son of Francis, purchased the property from Matilda Seaman in 1884. Wilhelmina died in 1911 and both are buried in the Old Paupack Cemetery.

Lewis Singer and his young wife, Frieda Buehler, found the house too small for their growing family and Lewis set about enlarging the home. He added rooms to the back of the house and added a second floor for more bedrooms. A summer kitchen was added to the back of the house.

Frieda Buehler Singer was born in Meimsheim, Wurtenberg, in 1860. She came to America with her parents in 1880. She and Lewis married in 1889. Six children were born to this couple: Harry, Laura, Clarence, Frederick (Pep), Edna, and Frances.

Lewis died in 1908 at the age of fifty-two. Frieda lived with her children until her death at the age of ninety. The farmhouse was retained by her third child, Clarence and his wife, Rose Gumble, until it was sold to William C. Gumble. Clarence replaced the large barn and added a two-story chicken coop and equipment building. An addition was put on the east side of the house and the summer kitchen was modernized to a permanent kitchen and laundry.

The present house has been remodeled extensively by its current owner, Kevin Brown, who lives there with his wife, Terri Gumble, a great, great-granddaughter of Francis Singer.

Figure 46 - Original Stone Foundation of Seaman Home

Figure 47 - Original Half-cut Logs Used as Joists in Seaman Home

FRASER SMITH - H.T. GUMBLE

Figure 48 - Frazer Smith - H. T. Gumble barn

Fraser Smith and his family occupied a 300-acre farm on the hill, east of the Singer and Seaman properties. In 1900, Henry and Elizabeth Gumble purchased the farm from the Smiths. This post and beam barn was on the Smith property. The farmhouse was razed in the mid-1920s and rebuilt. The frame house, the first house built by the fledging Gumble Brothers Company, remains today. It is owned by Henry's great, granddaughter.

The barn has undergone some modernization. The original manger was moved to the equipment room on the other side. The interior of the barn remains the same with hay mows and wooden ladders. The post and beam construction is evident. It appears to be one of the three remaining post and beam barns in the Township.

QUICK - GOBLE

Figure 49 - Alva Quick-Goble Home - 1919

The house pictured above is not actually old enough to be included in this book of nineteenth century homes. The present house was a Montgomery Ward package house, erected in 1919 on the site of the former house that had burned. However, the property of Alva Quick does meet the criteria because of the outbuildings still found on the property.

Figure 50 - Original Quick's Machine Shed

Alva Quick was the grandson of Simeon Quick and son of Samuel Quick who were mentioned as farmers in the Agricultural Census. The Quicks owned several farms. Their name appears on the river flats of Tafton and land located between the present-day ski run and Route # 6.

According to the Beers Map of 1872, this larger portion of the farm was located in Blooming Grove Township. Alva Quick purchased the land from John and Mary Jackson. John and Mary Jackson purchased the land from Westbrooks, a landed family in Blooming Grove Township. Most of the Jackson farm was located in Blooming Grove Township. A smaller portion of the property extended into Big Pond (Fairview Lake). John Jackson had only one horse, fourteen acres of improved land and raised corn, buckwheat, and potatoes.

The Jacksons broke up the property and sold to several people. The Quick family owned several farms in Palmyra Towship. Alva Quick, his wife, Laura and his only son, Harry, worked the farm. Harry remained on the farm until his death in 1963. He, along with several of his grandfather's family, is buried in the Old Paupack Cemetery.

Most of the land used for crops is on a higher plane behind the house and barn. The land of the original farm, lying mostly across the road to Promised Land (RT 390), is fully re-forested and difficult to trace as a one-time farm.

The barn or equipment shed shown below has a workshop with a loft over it and an area for wagon storage.

SIMPSON - ROBINSON

Figure 51 - Main View of Robinson Home

The land known as the Robinson Farm extends on both sides of the Promised Land Road or today's State Route 390. At one time the property encompassed the pond known as Lake Winona or Robinson's Pond. There are two houses shown on the Beers Map on this property in 1872: one is close to the road and the other house was located down the hill on the other side of the stone wall. This second house no longer exists.

William and Elizabeth Simpson and their two children were living on this farm in the 1850 Census records. Thomas and Mary Gouldin Robinson purchased the land from the Simpson. They had twin boys, George Henry and John.

The Robinsons moved into the farmhouse located nearer the to road.

A summer kitchen was attached to the larger two-story structure. A privy was located about thirty feet from the back door, covered by a grape arbor from door to door. Several outbuildings were constructed on the farm.

It is not known how long John remained on the farm, but George, now married to Tarressa, took over the property. George and Tarressa had twin sons, George and Thomas.

Figure 52 - View of Privy at Robinson Home

Thomas remained on the homestead with his elderly mother. Thomas married Dorothy Stevens and the couple had one, James, who is the current owner of the property. George and his wife, Elizabeth, located further north of the homestead. They had five children. Elizabeth was one of the Tafton Postmasters for many years.

Figure 53 - Side View of Summer Kitchen

LYNN-KETTERING

Figure 54 - Front View of Lynn Home

The Commemorative Biographical Record tells us much about the Lynn House and owner, Michael Lynn, who was one of the most successful farmers and entrepreneurs of Palmyra Township. As early as the tenth century, the Lynn family lived in County Mayo, Ireland, owners of a large tract of land and dealers in cattle. Although a Protestant family, the Lynns supported the Church of England and received large tracts of land from the King in reward for their loyalty. Nevertheless, the boys in the family married Catholic girls who were their neighbors and the families became staunch Catholics.

Michael J. Lynn came to America at the age of nineteen in 1854. He had about twenty dollars. He came to Hawley and worked on the coal dumps and the Pittston coal mines. After a lengthy stay in Chicago where he sold cattle, he returned to Palmyra Township and purchased his farm in 1864. His home was a two-story colonial with wrap-around porches on all four sides. He dealt in cattle for fifteen years and retired to become a butcher, leaving him time to cultivate over 100 acres to become the largest grain grower in the county. He also lumbered the remaining 100 acres, selling chestnut trees to be used as telephone poles.

Miss Theresa Lynn, granddaughter of Michael, spoke about her grandfather in the oral history taken in March of 2002. She said," Michael Lynn was well-liked. He assisted families arriving in Scranton from his native County Mayo by loading his wagon with goods, visiting them and finding them shelter and employment. He also employed orphans from St. Michael's Orphanage in Scranton to work summers on his farm. The money they earned would give them a start in life once they left the orphanage." In the 1870 Agricultural Census, Michael Lynn reported that he harvested 200 bushels of oats, 60 bushels of buckwheat, 250 bushels of Irish potatoes, and 250 pounds of butter.

Michael Lynn was a conservationist, according to Miss Lynn. He planted a tree for every tree cut down, used rain water for the household and crops, and rotated his crops. Accumulating considerable wealth, he founded the Hawley Bank in 1911.

On July 16, 1894, his home burned. Michael quickly rebuilt the larger house seen today, although it took the present owners to create the "pink lady of Palmyra Township". Lynn and his wife, Margaret Heley, had six sons and nine daughters. Three children died in childhood. The new home had a large kitchen and thirteen bedrooms.

After the home was sold out of the family, it passed through several hands. Victor Lurie, a producer, bought the house in the 1970s and he is credited with saving the house from destruction. Later owners attempted to renovate the house, but it took Scott and Debra Kettering to create the beautiful home that we see today. The Ketterings researched the colors of paint used for a house of this vintage and they selected several tones of pink. They tackled the splendid moldings in the house that had been badly damaged. Carefully working on each room and researching the wallpaper, paint and furnishings, they created a wonderful restoration with modern porches and living space.

Figure 55 - View of Half of the Front Parlor in Lynn Home

The one end of the parlor is shown here. The other side, with the bowed window, contains a grand piano.

Figure 56 - An Upstairs Bedroom Showing Heirloom Furniture

The front bedroom shown below, on the right, contains a bedstead used by the Kettering family for six generations.

Figure 57 - Another Bedroom in the Lynn Home

Shown here is a second upstairs bedroom

With the house mostly completed, the owners are concentrating on the front gardens and restoring the artesian well.

BINGHAM-KILLAM-SIMONS

Figure 58 - View of Bingham-Simons Home

Lot 26, next to the Chapman's Lot 25, was claimed by Hezekiah Bingham who was 37 years old when he arrived from Connecticut with the original settlers. Hezekiah was married to Phoebe Chapman, sister of Uriah Chapman, another of the original settlers. He and Phoebe lived on Lot 26 with their family of three sons and five daughters. Hezekiah died September 17, 1811, at the age of 74. During his lifetime, Hezekiah purchased considerable property. His holdings were divided among his sons: Hezekiah, Jr., Soloman, and Rudolphus.

Hezekiah, Jr. settled upon Lot 29 and purchased Lot 31 from Stephen Parrish in 1812. Rudolphus purchased Lot 28 which originally had been surveyed for Abisha Woodward, son of Enos Woodward. He married Sally Kimble, whose father, Jacob, owned Lot 30

The Bingham farm was purchased by Henry D. Clark in 1862. Clark gave an acre of his farm to be used as the Old Paupack Cemetery. In older records, this land is sometimes referred to as Bingham Cemetery. The long hill on the road to Hawley was called Bingham's Hill for some time as well. His son-in- law, Edwin Killam and daughter, Emily, bought the northeastern section of the property in 1878. The property passed to their daughter, Ida May and her husband, Leonard Simons. The Simons children remain as the owners of the property.

REFERENCES

Killam, Ephraim . The History of the Wallenpaupack Settlement

Matthews. History of the Counties of Wayne, Pike, and Monroe

Coutts, Donal C. Palmyra Township, Pike County. Pennsylvania-
A History,2007

1872 Beers Map of Palmyra Township, Pike County

Brown, Nan Coutts. History of the Pellett House

Vilardi, Thomas. History of the Ansley House

Graybill, Audrey. The Family of Gumble 2000

United States Population Census: 1850-1930

United States Agricultural Census 1850-1870

Stillwell Map of Wallenpaupack 1912

Pike County Deeds, Wills, and Land Transfers; Admin. Bldg Office of Recorder of Deed, Milford, PA

Original deeds of Francis Singer 1850

Original deeds of Conrad Gumble 1852

Ancestry.com genealogical records

LDS Family Search genealogical record

INDIVIDUAL CONTRIBUTORS

Darryl Box
Kevin Brown
Nan Coutts Brown
Meta Buehler
Virginia Buehler
Donal C. Coutts
George and Christine Coutts
Basil and Tara DeFranco
Janet Ansley Fucci
Arthur Goble
Sylvia Gumble Gregor
Girard Gumble
Nancy Killam Gumble
Jean Gumble Hansen
Scott and Debra Kettering
Marilyn Simons Lyman
Dennis and Joyce Manhart
Jill and Pete Porter
Raymond Rega
Margaret and Mark Reidenbach
James Robinson
Fred (JR) Singer, Jr.
Thomas and Lisa Vilardi

ORAL HISTORIES
(from the Wallenpaupack Historical Society Collections)

Albert Coutts

Teresa Lynn

Helen Killam Teeter

INDEX

Ansley
  John, 25
  Jonas, 19, 26
  Joseph, 26
Ansley Road, 18
Atkinson
  Joseph, 2, 33
Beam
  Augusta, 44
Bennett
  Augusta Beam, 44
  Isaac K., 44
  Jared, 44
  Lebbius, 44
  Mary Gates, 43
  Stephen, 43, 44
Big Pond, 74
Bingham
  Hezekiah, 16, 51, 87
  Hezekiah, Jr., 87
  Nancy, 16
  Phoebe Chapman, 87
  Rudolphus, 51, 87
  Soloman, 87
Box
  Darryl, 66
  Erma Singer, 66
Brown
  Jacob, 42
  Kevin, 69
  Nan Coutts, 16
Buehler
  Christof, 30, 33
  Frieda, 68
  Katherine, 30, 33
  Louise Timmerman, 33
  Paul, 34
  Scott, 34
  Virginia, 34
  Wilhelmina, 30
  William, 33
Buehler's Pond, 33
Bundy
  Abby, 25
  Abigail, 11
  Eunice, 25
Chapman
  Phoebe, 87
  Rachel Willis, 47
  Uriah, 47
  William, 47
Clark
  Emily, 88
  Henry D., 88
Coletto
  William, 3
Coutts
  Anna Gumble, 44
  George, 18, 44
  George, Jr., 44
  Harold, 18
  Helen, 45
  Robert, 45
CWDJS Associates, 48

Darby
  Bertha, 64
  Earle, 64
Duffy
  Michael, 6
Edwards
  Carol Kimble, 44
  Henry, 44
Ehrhardt's Restaurant, 64
Frank
  Auguste Berthe, 61
Gates
  Mary, 43
  Nathaniel, 43
Gessner
  Annie, 58
Goshen, NY, 15
Gouldin
  Mary, 77
Grathwohl
  Anna, 44
Gumble
  Anna, 44
  Anna Burn, 53
  Anna Burn Kimble, 6
  Anna Grathwohl, 44
  Annie Gessner, 58
  Barbara Kastler, 58
  Charles, 64
  Charles Conrad, 58
  Clyde, 10
  Conrad, 8, 44, 51, 52
  Conrad, Jr., 44
  Dorothea, 9, 53
  Dorthea, 8
  Edith, 59
  Elizabeth, 71
  Elizabeth Snell, 64
  Emil, 6
  Esther Singer, 64
  Eugenia, 10
  Henry, 54, 71
  Henry T., 9, 53, 64
  Hermann, 57
  Jack, 10
  Jeanette, 10
  Marie, 59
  Rose, 69
  Terri, 69
  William C., 69
Gumbletown, 53
Hanna, 33
Hansen
  Jean Gumble, 2
Hardenberg
  Edmund, 17
  Susan Pellett, 17
Haskel
  Jonathan, 43
Heley
  Margaret, 82
Indian Trail, 16
Jackson
  John, 74
  Mary, 74
Kastler
  Barbara, 58
Kettering
  Debra, 82
  Scott, 82
Killam, xiii, 1, 89, 91
  Alfred E., 5
  Asher, 5
  Benjamin F., 18
  Benjamin T., 1
  Clay, 48

Dan D., 47
　　Edwin, 88
　　Eliza, 6
　　Emily Clark, 88
　　Ephraim, 1, 11
　　George N., 12
　　Harriet, 5
　　Hellen, 48
　　Ida May, 88
　　Lucy, 48
　　Marcus Napoleon
　　　　Bonaparte, 2
　　Margaret Rohrbacker, 47
　　Moses, 1, 5, 48
　　Moses Jr., 47
　　Nancy, 7
　　Powell, 5
　　Silas, 1
　　Zadoc, 1
Killam.
　　Frances Hollister, 18
Kimble
　　Andrew Jackson, 8, 19
　　Arthur, 8
　　Carol, 44
　　Eunice, 19
　　Helen Pellett, 19
　　Hermann N., 29
　　Jacob, 87
　　Jacob, Jr., 25, 29
　　Nancy Pellett, 19
　　Sally, 87
Lester
　　Phineas, 15
Lurie
　　Victor, 82
Lynn
　　Margaret Heley, 82
　　Michael, 81
　　Theresa, 82
Maeder
　　Amelia, 3
Mahling
　　Amelia, 3
　　Jacob, 3
Mansuy
　　Alma Vetterlein, 31
Mill Brook, 33, 47, 51
Minisink/Wyoming Trail, 16
Nemanie Lodge, 44
Parrish
　　Stephen, 87
Peifer
　　Lizzie, 6
Pellett
　　Calvin, 17
　　Elizabeth, 15
　　Eunice Kimble, 18
　　Guerdon, 17, 18
　　John, 15
　　John, Jr., 15
　　Samuel, 41
　　Theodore, 18
　　William, 15
Probst
　　Alfred, 3
　　Edward, 3
Quick
　　Alva, 73
　　Harry, 75
　　Laura, 75
　　Samuel, 74
　　Simeon, 74
Red School, 12
Rega
　　Raymond, 38

Reidenbach
  Margaret, 64
  Mark, 64
Robinson
  Mary Gouldin, 77
  Thomas, 77
Rohrbacker
  Margaret, 47
Seaman, 64
  Helen, 68
  Jacob, 61, 67, 68
  Matilda, 68
  Wilhelmina, 68
Sheridan Stream, 51
Shive
  Franklin, 59
Simons
  Ida May Killam, 88
  Leonard, 88
Simpson
  Elizabeth, 77
  William, 77
Singer
  August, 66
  Auguste Berthe Frank, 61
  Charles, 64
  Clarence, 68
  Edna, 68
  Erma, 66
  Esther, 64
  Frances, 68
  Francis, 52, 61, 65, 67
  Frederick (Pep), 68
  Frieda Buehler, 68
  Harry, 68
  Laura, 68
  Lewis, 61, 68
  Martha M., 66
  Rose Gumble, 69
  William, 64
Slocum
  Joseph, 21
Slocum House, 9
Smith
  Fraser, 71
  Nora Del, 9, 53
Snell
  Elizabeth, 64
Steinman
  Margaret, 42
Timmerman
  Louise, 33
Vetterlein
  Frederike, 29
  Henry, 29
  Walter, 30
Vilardi
  Lisa, 26
  Tom, 26
Warner
  Hetty, 19
  Peter, 19
Weill
  Henry, 18
Widner
  Samuel, 41
Williams
  Charles, 48
  Lucy Killam, 48
  Ralph, 48
Willis
  Rachel, 47
Wissling, 64
  Casper, 65
  Magdelena, 65
Witter

Elizabeth, 2
Wohlfart
  Ethel, 64
Woodward
  Abisha, 87
  Enos, 87

Sally Kimble, 87
Zimmerman
  Elsie, 41
  Jacob, 38, 41
  John, 38, 41
  Margaret Steinman, 42